MW00938113

Mr. McFunny's Soccer Jokes for Kids

Richard Seidman
Illustrations by Curt Evans

Catalyst Group ◉ Ashland, Oregon

Mr. McFunny's Soccer Jokes for Kids / Richard Seidman.
First edition

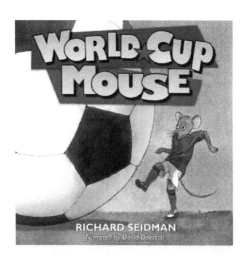

Free Bonus: *World Cup Mouse* Audiobook

Hey folks! If you'd like to listen to the audiobook version of another funny book, *World Cup Mouse*, you can download it for **FREE** by clicking on the link below.

"Where there's a mouse, there's a way!" says Louie LaSurie. But it will take more than lofty words for Louie to achieve his goal: to be the first mouse to play for France in the World Cup soccer tournament. Can he do it? Find out in the *World Cup Mouse* audiobook.

Get it for **FREE** at www.richardseidman.com/free-bonus-world-cup-mouse-audio-book

Introducing Mr. McFunny

Hello, my name is Maximillian McFunny. My friends call me Mr. McFunny. I love jokes. I have ever since I was a little McFunny.

Another thing I love is sports. Playing them and watching them. Especially soccer, football, basketball, baseball, volleyball, track and field, swimming, biking, hockey, cricket, badminton, wrestling, jai alai, pickleball, curling, jacks... Well, you get the picture.

So when my niece, Matilda McFunny, suggested I compile a series of sports joke books for kids, I jumped at the idea. The only problem was the ceiling was too low.

I'm always on the lookout for new jokes or even good, old ones, so if you have a sports joke to share, please send it to me at <u>jokes@mcfunnybooks.com</u>. Everyone who submits a sports joke will be entered in a monthly drawing to receive a Mr. McFunny book for free.

Each month, I'll choose my favorite jokes to post on my website with the senders' names.

Thanks for reading this book. I hope you enjoy it. And that's no joke.

Laughingly yours,
Maximillian McFunny

Kickoff: Let the Jokes Begin!

Where was the first World Cup held?
In the hands of the winners.

Which soccer player keeps the field neat?
The sweeper.

What player brings the goalposts and net home after every game?
The goalkeeper.

What do soccer referees send to their friends during the holidays?
Yellow cards.

Why do lots of Brazilian soccer players go by a single name, like Pele or Neymar or Hulk?
It would be too confusing if they went by ten names.

Coach: Why didn't you stop the ball?
Goalie: I thought that's what the net was for.

What's the difference between an opera star and a brand new soccer stadium?
One is pitch perfect and the other has perfect pitch.*

* "Pitch" is another word for a soccer field.

Maria: Are you a good soccer player?
Alex: Good? I'm so good I can play without using my hands.

How can you keep a mule from kicking?
Take away his soccer ball.

What do you call a soccer team's lunch in the park?
A kick-nic.

What do you call a defender who just ate a big meal?
A fullback.

Why do people play soccer?
For kicks.

Who's the sloppiest player in soccer history?
Lionel Messy.*

Lionel Messi plays for the Argentine national team and for his club, Barcelona. He is considered one of the greatest soccer players of all time.

What runs around a soccer field but never moves?
A fence.

Who's the best player in soccer history?
George Best.*

George Best starred with Manchester United and the Northern Ireland National Team in the 1960s, '70s, and early '80s.

Why didn't the dog want to play soccer?
He was a boxer.

Why didn't the team want to play with a third soccer ball?
Because it was an oddball.

There was a goalkeeper called Walter
Who played on the island of Malta,
But his kicks were so long
And the wind was so strong,
That the ball ended up in Gibraltar.

Why did the boss play soccer in his bare feet?
Because he had given his employee the boot.

Why do soccer players do so well in school?
They know how to use their heads.

Why was Cinderella kicked off her soccer team?
She kept running away from the ball.

Why was Cinderella so bad at soccer tactics?
She had a pumpkin for a coach.

What's the difference between a human soccer player and a dog?
A human wears a full uniform, but a dog only pants.

Why did the coach start a one-year-old on his team?
The kid was good at dribbling.

What did the soccer ball say to the player?
I get a kick out of you.

What soccer player is good to have on your team when you're playing Scrabble?
Xavi.*

* Xavi, whose full name is Xavier Hernández Creus, helped Spain win the World Cup in 2010. In Scrabble, the letter "X" is worth eight points.

Why do tuna not make good goalies?
They keep getting caught in the net.

Why was it so hot in the soccer stadium after the game?
All the fans had left.

Where do teams go to replace their old soccer shirts?
New Jersey.

What is a ghost's favorite soccer position?
Ghoulkeeper.

What kind of tea do reckless soccer players drink?
Penal-tea.

What soccer player is never promoted?
The left back.

What's black and white and looks like a soccer ball?
A soccer ball.

What's it called when a dinosaur gets a goal?
A dino-score.

What do you call rowdy soccer fans who live near the Grinch who stole Christmas?
Who-ligans.*

Hooligans are rowdy soccer fans who get in fights and cause trouble before, during, and after soccer matches. Who-ville is a fictional town created by the author Dr. Seuss and featured in his book, How the Grinch Stole Christmas.*

What lights up the soccer stadium?
A match.

Why do artists never win when they play soccer?
Because they keep drawing.

Why did the soccer player carry string when she was subbed into the game?
So she could tie the match.

What part of a soccer stadium is never the same?
The changing room.

Why did the goalpost get angry?
Because the crossbar was rattled.

What should a soccer team do if the field is flooded?
Bring on their subs.

What Dutch star sounds like a thief?
Arjen Robben.*

Arjen Robben played for the German club, Bayern Munich, and also for the Netherlands National Team.)

Why are soccer stadiums strange?
Because you can sit in the stands, but you can't stand in the sits.

Where do churchgoers practice soccer?
The prayground.

Where do soccer players go to dance?
The soccer ball.

Hector: Our team is tied for first place in the league. We're undefeated and no one's scored against us.
Victor: Wow! How many games have you played?
Hector: None. The season starts on Saturday.

Which goalkeepers can jump higher than the crossbar?
All of them. Crossbars can't jump.

Where do you go in Spain when you're tired of seeing mirages?
Real Madrid.*

Real Madrid is a professional soccer team based in Madrid, Spain.

What position did the union leader play?
Striker.

What American soccer star of the 1980s and '90s would make a great actress?
Mia Hamm.*

Mia Hamm is a two-time Olympic gold medalist and World Cup winner with the U.S. Women's National Team.

What was it called when Mia was boxed in between two defenders?
A Hamm sandwich.

What did Mia's teammates have for a pre-game breakfast?
Eggs with Hamm.

Why did Mia climb to the top of the goal post?
She was Hamming it up.

How is a referee like Snow White in the Walt Disney movie, *Snow White and the Seven Dwarfs*?
They both whistle while they work.

When does a soccer player not need any money?
When she has a free kick.

Who's the greatest soccer-playing whale in history?
Moby Kick.

Why did the grass have to leave the soccer team?
It was cut.

Why was the centipede dropped from the soccer team?
He took too long to put on his cleats.

What's the difference between a soccer shoe and a trombone?
One's a boot and the other's a toot.

Why did the silly defender throw fishing gear at the striker?
To tackle him.

How do hens cheer their soccer teams?
They egg them on.

What soccer player is due to reappear on the field at any moment?
Right back.

Why did the chicken get a yellow card?
Because of fowl play.

What did the referee tell Zinedine Zidane about the rules?
No butts about it.*

* Zinedine Zidane led France to victory in the 1998 World Cup, and was kicked out of the final match of the 2006 World Cup for head-butting an Italian opponent.)

Why did the tiny ghost join the soccer squad?
He heard they needed a little team spirit.

Why did the manager bring a suitcase to the game?
So she could pack the defense.

What's the difference between a duck and a dishonest striker?
One flaps and the other flops.

Why did the coach give his players lighters?
Because they kept losing their matches.

What Brazilian star of the 2000s has the most embarrassing name?
Kaká.

What's Kaká's last name?
Poo-poo.

A man arrives at a soccer match midway through the second half.
"What's the score?" he asks.
"Zero to zero," someone replies.
The first man asks, "And what was the score at half-time?"

Paul: What jersey should I buy?
Mary: Buy a goalie's jersey.
Paul: Why?
Mary: That way, I can tell everyone my boyfriend's a keeper.

A player who turned out for Dover
Had no shirt, so he wore a pullover,
But the thing was too long,
And he put it on wrong,
So that all he could do was fall over.

Why did the referee have such a high phone bill?
Because he made so many calls.

Why did the soccer field end up as a triangle?
Someone took a corner.

Reasons to be a referee:
- You love soccer, but can't quite understand the rules.
- You have a strange desire to run aimlessly around in the wind, rain, and snow.
- You love the sound of verbal abuse.
- You find it hard to make decisions, and whenever you do you're always wrong.

Humpty Dumpty dribbled the ball.
Humpty Dumpty had a great fall.
And the referee booked him for diving.

Why did the soccer player hold her shoe to her ear?
Because she loved sole music.

What did the midfielder do when he saw a girl he liked?
He made a pass.

Joe: For a moment, our team had a good chance.
Flo: Then what happened?
Joe: The game started.

The End

Send Mr. McFunny
Your Favorite Sports Jokes

Know any other funny soccer jokes? Please send your jokes to me at jokes@mcfunnybooks.com. Everyone who submits a soccer or other sports joke will be entered in a monthly drawing to receive a free Mr. McFunny e-book. And each month, I'll select my favorite jokes to post on my website, along with the senders' names.

If you like this Mr. McFunny book, please do me a favor and leave a review *on Amazon*.

Please check out my other Mr. McFunny Sports Joke Books for Kids www.amazon.com /-/e/B001IXS50A.

Bye for now!

Funnily yours,
Maximillian McFunny

Team McFunny

In addition to creating the Mr. McFunny books, author **Richard Seidman** wrote *World Cup Mouse* and several screenplays for family films. He lives in Ashland, Oregon, USA with his wife and chickens and many stuffed animals.

Illustrator, **Curt Evans**, started cartooning as a kid...and never stopped. His drawings have appeared in books, on the sides of city buses, and on more than a hundred T-shirt designs.

Maximillian McFunny, known as "Mr. McFunny" to his friends, is a compiler of jokes, riddles, puns, and limericks on sports and other subjects such as toilet bowls. He lives in the state of Imagination along with his many pets and his wife, Mrs. McFunny.

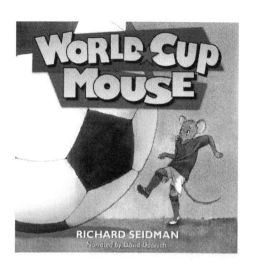

Free Bonus: *World Cup Mouse* Audiobook

Hey folks! If you'd like to listen to the audiobook version of another funny book, *World Cup Mouse*, you can download it for **FREE** by clicking on the link below.

"Where there's a mouse, there's a way!" says Louie LaSurie. But it will take more than lofty words for Louie to achieve his goal: to be the first mouse to play for France in the World Cup soccer tournament. Can he do it? Find out in the *World Cup Mouse* audiobook.

Get it for **FREE** at www.richardseidman.com/ free-bonus-world-cup-mouse-audio-book

18382050R00022

Printed in Poland
by Amazon Fulfillment
Poland Sp. z o.o., Wrocław